100 facts
STARS & GALAXIES

100 facts

STARS & GALAXIES

Clive Gifford

Consultant: Sue Becklake

Miles
KeLLY

First published in 2015 by Miles Kelly Publishing Ltd
Harding's Barn, Bardfield End Green, Thaxted, Essex, CM6 3PX, UK

2 4 6 8 10 9 7 5 3 1

PUBLISHING DIRECTOR Belinda Gallagher
CREATIVE DIRECTOR Jo Cowan
EDITORIAL DIRECTOR Rosie Neave
EDITOR Fran Bromage
DESIGNERS Andrea Slane, Rob Hale
IMAGE MANAGER Liberty Newton
INDEXER Jane Parker
PRODUCTION Elizabeth Collins, Caroline Kelly
REPROGRAPHICS Stephan Davis, Jennifer Cozens, Thom Allaway

ISBN 978-1-78209-648-1

Printed in China

British Library Cataloguing-in-Publication Data
A catalogue record for this book is available from the British Library

ACKNOWLEDGEMENTS
The publishers would like to thank the following artists who have contributed to this book:
Mike Foster (Maltings Partnership), Stuart Jackson-Carter, Alex Pang, Rudi Vizi
All other artwork from the Miles Kelly Artwork Bank

The publishers would like to thank the following sources for the use of their photographs:
Key: t = top, b = bottom, l = left, r = right, c = centre, bg = background, ut = used throughout
Cover: (front) Mark Garlick/Science Photo Library; (back, t) John A Davis/Shutterstock.com
(back, cl) Markus Gann/Shutterstock.com; (back, cr) NASA/JPL-Caltech/R. Hurt (SSC)
ALMA 43(b) (ESO/NAOJ/NRAO), C.Padilla Corbis 38(tr) Blue Lantern Studio; 40–41(bg) Stapleton Collection
European Space Agency 10(tr) ESA/Hubble & NASA, Judy Schmidt; 11(tr) ESA–D.Ducros, 2013, (cl) ESA/Hubble & NASA;
13(tr) NASA, ESA & Hubble Heritage Team (AURA/STScI), (br) J.P. Harrington (University of Maryland) and K.J. Borkowski (NCSU) and NASA;
19(bl) NASA, ESA and H. Bond (STScI); 22–23(bg) ESA Adrienne Cool (SFSU) et al., Hubble Heritage Team (STScI/AURA), NASA; 27(c) NASA/
ESA/J.Hester and A.Loll (Arizona State Univ.); 28(c) NASA/Dana Berry; 32(c) NASA, ESA, and the Hubble Heritage Team (STScI/AURA)-ESA/
Hubble Collaboration; 33(b) ESA/Herschel/PACS/MESS Key Programme Supernova Remnant Team, NASA, ESA and Allison Loll/Jeff Hester
(Arizona State University); 44(c) ESA/NASA/ Geneva University Observatory(Frederic Pont) iStock 12(bl) duncan1890
Paul & Kathryn Gray 27(bl) Max Starmus NASA 5(tr) Northrop Grumman, (b) NASA/Dana Berry, (tl) NASA/JPL-Caltech; 12(c) Subaru
Telescope (NAOJ), Hubble Space Telescope, Martin Pugh, Robert Gendler; 13(cr) Joseph Brimacombe/NASA; 14(c) John MacKenty (STScI) et al.
& the Hubble Heritage Team (AURA/ STScI/ NASA); 15(b) NASA/JPL-Caltech, (bl) NASA, JPL-Caltech, WISE; 24–25(bg) NASA/CXC/M.Weiss;
25(cl) NASA/JPL-Caltech; 26(bl) NASA, ESA, Zolt Levay (StScI); 29(c) NASA, (br) NASA/JPL-Caltech; 30(c) X-ray: NASA/UMass/D.Wang et al.,
IR: NASA/STScI, (br) Alain Riazuelo; 31(c) NASA/Goddard Space Flight Center/Swift; 33(tl) Y. Izotov (Main Astronomical Obs., Ukraine),
T. Thuan (Univ. Virginia), ESA, NASA; 33(b) NASA/CXC/JPL-Caltech/STScI, (bl) NASA/STScI/SAO, (bl) NASA/JPL-Caltech/GSFC, (bl) NASA/JPL-
Caltech, (bl) NASA/JPL-Caltech, (bl) NASA/JPL-Caltech, (bl) NASA/JPL-Caltech/SAO/NOAO, (bl) NASA/CXC/JPL-Caltech/STScI/NSF/NRAO/
VLA, (bl) NASA/JPL-Caltech/ESA/Harvard-Smithsonian CfA; 34–35(bg) Star Shadows Remote Observatory and PROMPT/CTIO (Steve Mazlin,
Jack Harvey, Rick Gilbert, and Daniel Verschatse); 34(cl) Canada-France-Hawaii Telescope, J.-C. Cuillandre (CFHT), Coelum; 35(cr) Local Group
Galaxies Survey Team, NOAO, AURA, NSF, (c) NASA, ESA, Hubble Heritage Team (STScI/AURA) Hubble Heritage (STScI/AURA) L. Jenkins
(GSFC/U. Leicester); 39(tr) Northrop Grumman; 42(tr) NASA CXC/NGST, (br) X-ray: NASA/CXC/UMass/D.Wang et al., Optical: NASA/HST/
D.Wang et al.; 43(cl) Ipac/Caltech/NASA, (c) NASA/JPL-Caltech/R. Hurt (SSC); 44(tr) NASA/Tim Pyle; 46(tr) NASA Ames/SETI Institute/JPL-
Caltech; 47(bl) NASA Science Photo Library 6(c) NASA/ESA/Hubble Heritage Team/STScI/AURA; 10(c) Detlev Van Ravenswaay; 12(bl) Sheila
Terry; 16–17(c) Science Picture Co.; 18(c) Babak Tafreshi; 20–21(c) Mark Garlick; 23(tr) Jose Antonio Penas; 36–37(bg) Mark Garlick;
38–39(bg) Alex Cherney, Terrastro.com; 42(bc) Carlos Clarivan; 44(bl) Detlev Van Ravenswaay; 45(tr) NASA, (br) Detlev Van Ravenswaay;
46(br) Nicolle R. Fuller; 47(tr) Eye of Science Shutterstock.com 1(b) Vadim Sadovski; 2(bg) Kevin Key; 6(tl, ut) R-studio; 8(cl, ut) Shutterstock,
(bc, ut) Andrey_Kuzmin, (tr, ut) Shawn Hine; 9(c) evv; 10(tr, ut) Aleksandr Bryliaev, (br, ut) Stephen Rees; 11(tl, ut) fluidworkshop; 12(bl) Margrit
Hirsch; 13(br, ut) caesart; 16(cl, ut) studio online; 23(tl) Valentin Agapov, (c) dedek; 25(t, ut) STILLFX; 26(cr, bg) Det-anan, (cr) Nicku;
34(bg) Popova Valeriya; 34(br, ut) 501room; 41(bl) Yganko; 46(br) Andrey_Kuzmin Topfoto 39(bl) The Granger Collection

All other photographs are from:
digitalSTOCK, digitalvision, John Foxx, PhotoAlto, PhotoDisc, PhotoEssentials, PhotoPro, Stockbyte

Every effort has been made to acknowledge the source and copyright holder of each picture.
Miles Kelly Publishing apologizes for any unintentional errors or omissions.

The publishers would like to thank the Society for Popular Astronomy for their help in compiling this book.

Made with paper from a sustainable forest

www.mileskelly.net   info@mileskelly.net

Contents

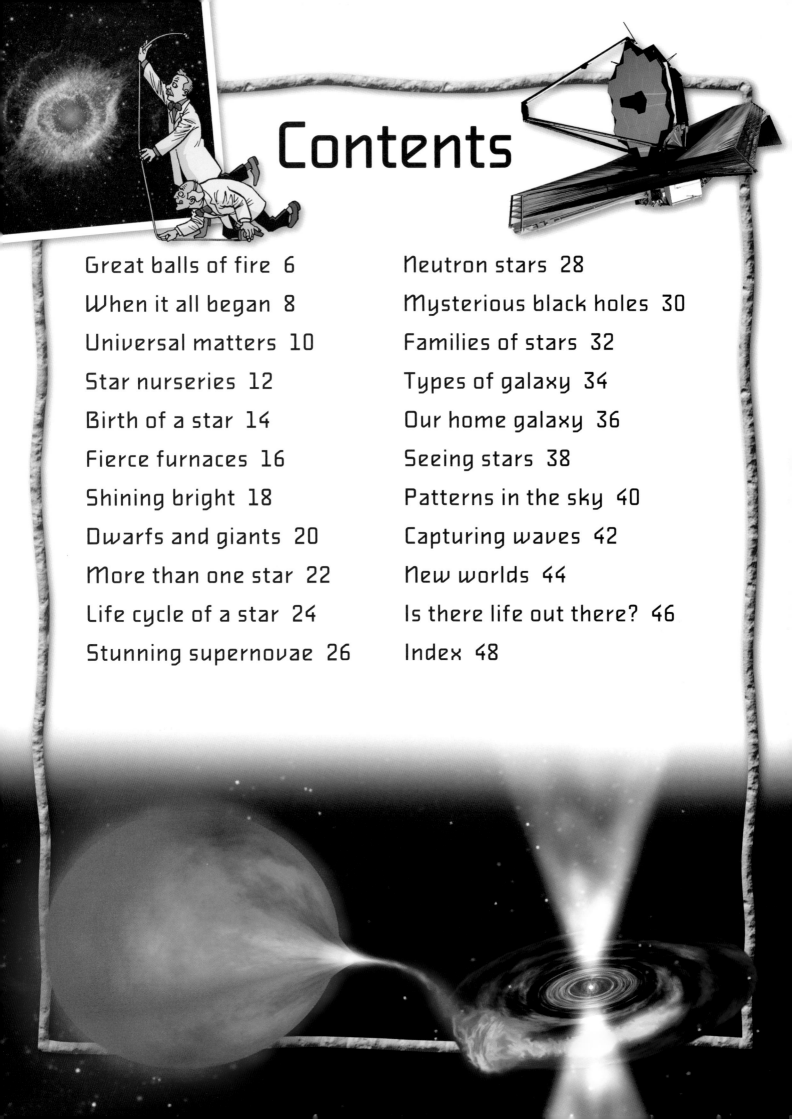

Great balls of fire

1 Stars are giant balls of very hot gas. These give off lots of heat as well as light, which allow us to see them in the sky. The stars we see at night are just a tiny fraction of the number found in the Universe. The National Observatory in London, UK estimates that there are around 70,000 million million million stars in the Universe.

▼ Stars are grouped together in large collections called galaxies. This image is part of the Large Magellanic Cloud, a neighbouring galaxy to our own galaxy, the Milky Way.

When it all began

2 The Universe is approximately 13.7 billion (thousand million) years old. If you squeezed down that time into a single 24-hour day, then the very first people on Earth didn't appear until the last minute.

3 Scientists believe the Universe began out of a single point. The theory of how the Universe began is often called the Big Bang, but it wasn't an explosion. Scientists believe that everything expanded out of a single point.

13.5 BILLION YEARS AGO

13.69 BILLION YEARS AGO

13.7 BILLION YEARS AGO

▲ Cosmic background radiation from the Big Bang is given out.

▲ The Universe continues to expand as the earliest stars form.

▲ Inflation from a single point was rapid with the Universe doubling its size at least a hundred times in a fraction of a second.

4 The first stars didn't form until 200 million years after the Big Bang. Millions more followed including our Sun, which formed almost 9 thousand million years later.

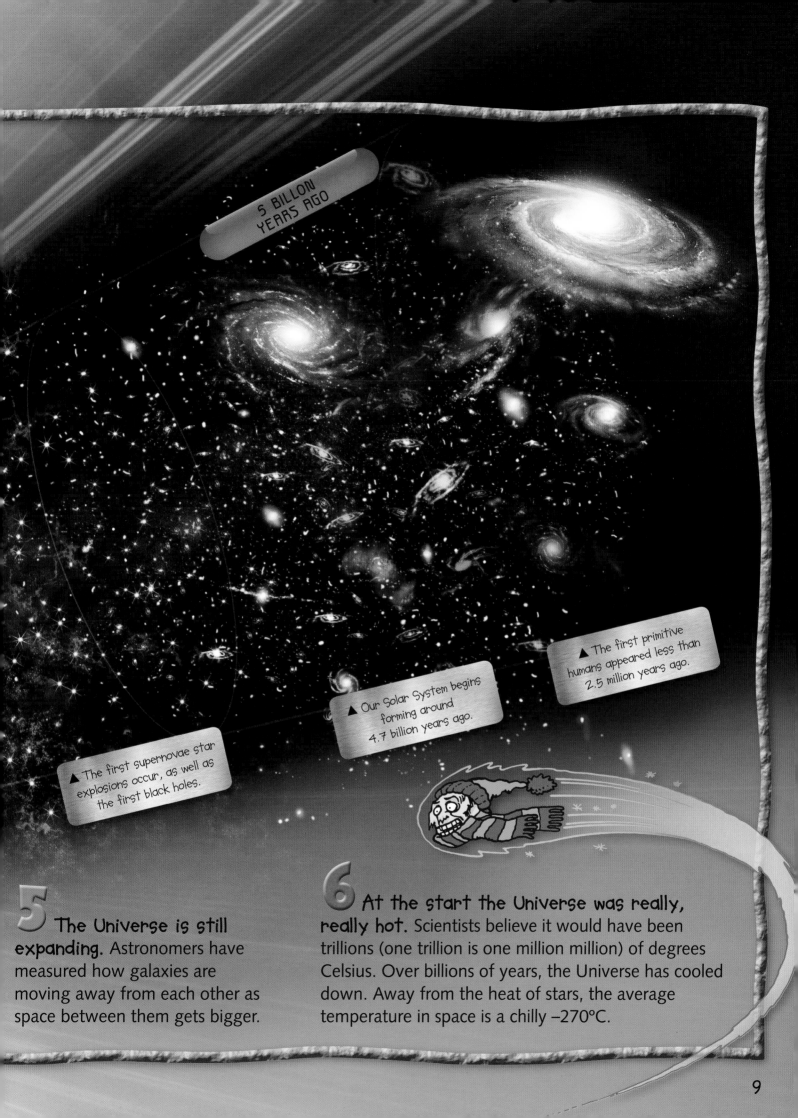

5 BILLION YEARS AGO

▲ The first supernovae star explosions occur, as well as the first black holes.

▲ Our Solar System begins forming around 4.7 billion years ago.

▲ The first primitive humans appeared less than 2.5 million years ago.

5 **The Universe is still expanding.** Astronomers have measured how galaxies are moving away from each other as space between them gets bigger.

6 **At the start the Universe was really, really hot.** Scientists believe it would have been trillions (one trillion is one million million) of degrees Celsius. Over billions of years, the Universe has cooled down. Away from the heat of stars, the average temperature in space is a chilly −270°C.

▼ Giant galaxies are so massive that their force of gravity may pull other, smaller, galaxies towards them.

7 Gravity is the invisible force attracting and holding stars and galaxies together. It pulls objects towards each other, and is what pulls you down on Earth's surface and stops you floating away. Gravity also keeps planets travelling in a path around a star like our Sun. This path is called an orbit.

▼ Eight planets are found in the Solar System. They all travel on elliptical paths as they orbit the Sun.

NEPTUNE

URANUS

MERCURY

EARTH

VENUS

MARS

8 Large objects have more gravity than smaller ones. The amount of 'stuff' an object contains is called its mass. Stars, like our Sun, have much more mass than planets so pull planets into orbit around them.

SATURN

JUPITER

NEAREST STARS TO EARTH

Proxima Centauri	4.2 light years
Alpha Cen A	4.4 light years
Alpha Cen B	4.4 light years
Barnard's Star	6.0 light years
CN Leo	7.8 light years

▶ Gaia satellite will measure how far away one billion stars are.

9 Light travels incredibly fast – at speeds of almost 299,792,458 metres per second. It can travel more than seven times around Earth in just a second. Scientists use the distance that light travels in one year to measure the huge distances in space. A single light year is 63,000 times the distance between Earth and the Sun.

DISTANCE LIGHT TRAVELS IN KILOMETRES

1 light second	299,792.5 km
1 light minute	17.98 million km
1 light day	25.9 billion km
1 light year	9.46 million million km

10 Launched in 2013, the Gaia satellite will measure how far away stars are from Earth. It is on a five-year mission and will build up a 3D map, measuring some of the stars' distances to within 0.001% accuracy.

11 When we view distant objects in the Universe, we are seeing how they looked in the past. Even though light travels really fast, it can take millions of years to reach us from a distant star or galaxy. What we see is how the object looked millions of years ago.

▶ Our Sun is our closest star at 149,600,000 km away. The next nearest star is Proxima Centauri. It is 4.2 light years away.

I DON'T BELIEVE IT!

In just over three years, Hipparcos – a satellite launched by ESA in 1989 – measured how far over a million different stars were from Earth.

Star nurseries

12 Stars are born in giant star nurseries called nebulae. Nebulae are giant clouds containing dust and gases, mostly hydrogen and some helium. Inside a nebula are all the elements needed to form new stars, called protostars.

▼ A single nebula can contain thousands of new stars. In 2005, the Spitzer telescope discovered 150 protostars never seen before in this Trifid Nebula.

13 There may be as many as 2500 nebulae in the Milky Way. Over the centuries, many astronomers have spotted nebulae. Brother and sister, William and Caroline Herschel performed a major search of the skies in the late 18th and early 19th centuries.

▲ Caroline Herschel became the first woman to discover a comet in 1786, whilst William Herschel built a 12 metre telescope three years later, the largest of its day.

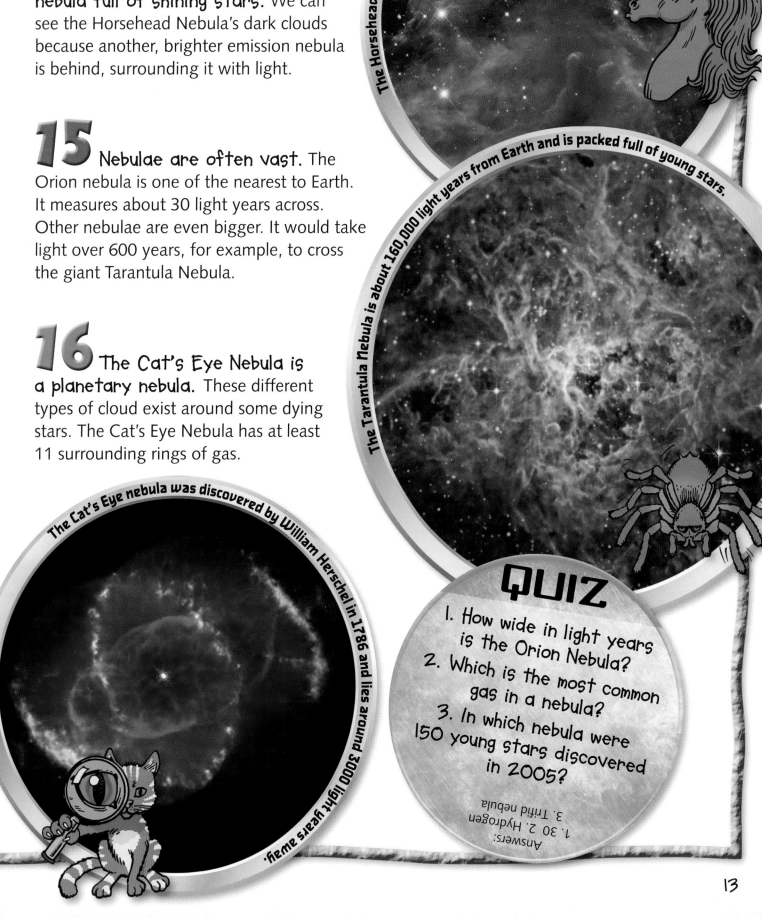

14 An emission nebula is a bright nebula full of shining stars. We can see the Horsehead Nebula's dark clouds because another, brighter emission nebula is behind, surrounding it with light.

15 Nebulae are often vast. The Orion nebula is one of the nearest to Earth. It measures about 30 light years across. Other nebulae are even bigger. It would take light over 600 years, for example, to cross the giant Tarantula Nebula.

16 The Cat's Eye Nebula is a planetary nebula. These different types of cloud exist around some dying stars. The Cat's Eye Nebula has at least 11 surrounding rings of gas.

The Horsehead Nebula is found in the Orion constellation and is 1500 light years from Earth.

The Tarantula Nebula is about 160,000 light years from Earth and is packed full of young stars.

The Cat's Eye nebula was discovered by William Herschel in 1786 and lies around 3000 light years away.

QUIZ

1. How wide in light years is the Orion Nebula?
2. Which is the most common gas in a nebula?
3. In which nebula were 150 young stars discovered in 2005?

Answers:
1. 30 2. Hydrogen 3. Trifid nebula

17 New stars, called protostars, form from clouds of gas and dust in a nebula. The dust and gas gets drawn together and becomes hotter and more dense. As the clump gets bigger and more tightly packed, its gravity increases. This force pulls in yet more dust and gas.

Clumps of gas in this nebula start to shrink into the tight round balls that will become stars.

The gas spirals round as it is pulled inwards. Any left-over gas and dust may form planets around the new star.

Deep in its centre, the new star starts making energy, but it is still hidden by the cloud of dust and gas.

The dust and gas are blown away and we can see the star shining. Maybe it has a family of planets like the Sun.

▼ The centre of the NGC 4214 galaxy contains hundreds of hot, young stars being formed. Many of these are less than two million years old.

18 A protostar can take 100,000 years to form. During this time, the clump grows and grows, drawing in more material. The middle of the clump is squeezed more and more tightly together so that it gets incredibly hot and pressurised.

19 Stars turn hydrogen gas into helium and energy. If the centre of a protostar gets hot enough, it will start nuclear fusion reactions, which use hydrogen as their fuel.

▼ NASA's Wide-field Infrared Survey Explorer (WISE) satellite has captured a multitude of stars and galaxies, including a brown dwarf (circled).

20 Some protostars never become proper stars because they don't get big enough. Instead, they gradually cool down and become a failed star, called a brown dwarf.

21 The coolest known star in the Universe is as cold as the North Pole on Earth. A brown dwarf, WISE J085510.83-071442.5 is estimated at −48°C to −13°C.

▲ This artist's impression shows a Y dwarf — a member of the brown dwarf family. They give off little heat and light, so are very hard to find in space.

I DON'T BELIEVE IT!
The core of a protostar needs to be 10 million°C before nuclear reactions occur — that's hot!

Fierce furnaces

22 **Stars are enormous furnaces generating vast amounts of energy.** In a star's centre, or core, lots of hydrogen gas is used to fuel powerful nuclear fusion reactions.

23 **The temperature in a star's core during its main sequence is unbelievably hot, about 15 million°C.** As a star nears the end of its life, the temperature in the core may increase.

24 **Nine out of ten stars spotted in the night sky burn hydrogen to form helium.** These stars are in their main sequence – the period in the life of a star after it has developed from a protostar. The main sequence lasts until the star runs out of hydrogen. The Sun is roughly halfway through its nine to ten billion year-long main sequence.

25 **Two forces keep the star approximately the same size during its main sequence.** The incredibly hot gas heated by the fusion reactions in the star's core presses outwards with huge force. This pressure is balanced by the star's gravity pulling gas in towards its centre.

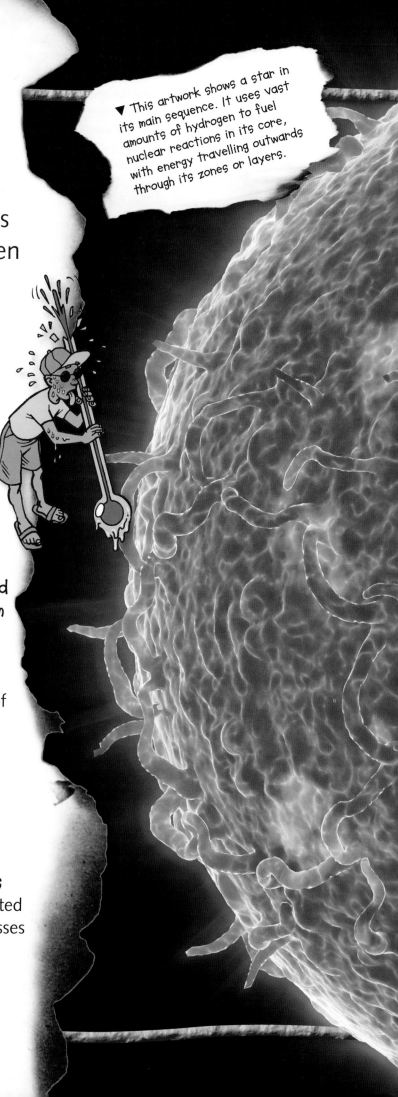

▼ This artwork shows a star in its main sequence. It uses vast amounts of hydrogen to fuel nuclear reactions in its core, with energy travelling outwards through its zones or layers.

26 Energy from the core of a star can take thousands of years to reach its surface. It journeys through the star's zones by either radiation or convection. In radiation, the energy travels in waves, like light. In convection, the energy travels on currents inside the star, a bit like really hot wind.

Energy moves outwards

Gravity pushes inwards

Convective zone

Radiative zone

Core

Photosphere

Dwarfs and giants

33 The most common type of stars are red dwarfs. They are less than half the size of the Sun and make up over two thirds of all stars. They burn their fuel more slowly than stars like the Sun, so they last as long as a trillion years.

32 Astronomers group stars together in different ways, including by size. At one end of the size scale are hypergiants and supergiants, like Antares. These stars can be 100 times bigger than the Sun and have relatively short lives because they burn their fuel so quickly.

Name: Antares
Spectral Type: M
Temp: Cool
Size: Red supergiant

Name: Rigel A
Spectral Type: B
Temp: Hot
Size: Blue giant

Name: Sirius A
Spectral Type: A
Temp: Hot
Size: Blue dwarf

34 Astronomers also group stars together by temperature. You may be used to thinking of blue for cold and red for hot, but the hottest stars, like Rigel, appear white-blue and the coolest stars look red.

SPECTRAL TYPE	COLOUR	TEMPERATURE
O		28,000–50,000°C
B		10,000–28,000°C
A		7500–10,000°C
F		6000–7500°C
G		5000–6000°C
K		3500–5000°C
M		2500–5500°C

35 The stellar spectral types range from O to M. Type O stars are the hottest with temperatures of 30,000°C or more. The Sun, with a surface temperature of 5500°C, is a type G star – in the middle. Type M stars, like Antares, are the coolest with temperatures below 3500°C.

▲ The Sun, Sirius A and Rigel A are all dwarfed by this massive star, Antares, which has a diameter over 880 times bigger than the Sun's.

Name: The Sun
Spectral Type: G
Temp: Medium
Size: Yellow dwarf

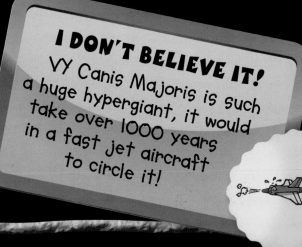

36 The fate of a star depends on its mass. For stars with a mass of more than three times the Sun, the ending is usually violent, involving a swelling in size before exploding as a supernova.

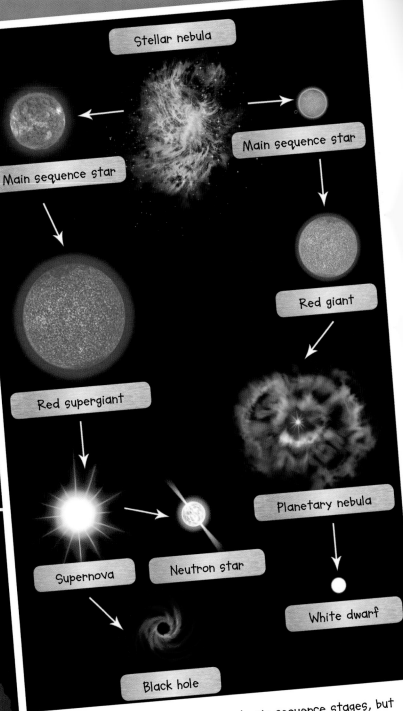

Stellar nebula

Main sequence star

Main sequence star

Red giant

Red supergiant

Planetary nebula

Supernova   Neutron star

White dwarf

Black hole

▲ Stars all go through protostar and main sequence stages, but their mass determines the stages after they run out of hydrogen in their core to use as fuel.

More than one star

37 Most stars in the Universe are not on their own. Our Sun is a lone star, but about a third of the stars in the Milky Way are part of a binary (two) or multiple (three plus) star system.

38 Binary stars are attracted by each other's force of gravity. The two stars travel round a point, called the centre of mass. This is like the balancing point on a see-saw and is often between the two stars.

▼ These binary stars orbit around a point between them. As one star is more massive than the other, the centre of mass is closer to it than the smaller star.

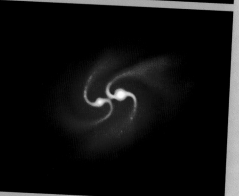
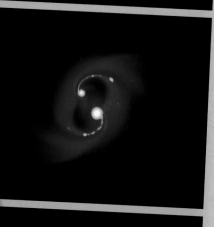

MAKE BINARY STARS

You will need:
pencil   piece of string
one large and one small ball of modelling clay

1. Push the balls on each end of the pencil and tie the string around its middle.
2. Dangle the pencil and balls and move the string along the pencil until the two balls balance.
3. Gently push one end of the pencil to see the two stars orbit round. The point where the string is tied is the common centre of mass between the two binary stars.

39 More than 1000 stars can be found in the Pleiades cluster, which is 440 light years away. It is made up of hot, bright, young stars and brown dwarfs, which shine dimly. Many ancient civilizations recognized this star cluster in the night sky.

▶ The Nebra Sky Disc is a 3600-year-old bronze disc found in Germany with gold insets showing the Sun, Moon and stars of the Pleiades cluster.

40 Some stars are found in large groups called open clusters. Many stars may form in the same area of a nebula at around the same time. At first, these stars stay close to each other before gradually drifting away.

◀ Some of the hot, young stars of the Pleiades open cluster shine brightly. Astronomers have found more than 1100 of these clusters in the Milky Way alone.

41 Globular clusters can contain hundreds of thousands of stars. These are large collections of mostly old stars found in the centre of a galaxy. Omega Centauri is a globular cluster containing 10 million stars.

▶ Many of these stars in Omega Centauri are millions of kilometres apart from each other.

Life cycle of a star

42 Stars don't last forever – they die when they run out of fuel. When a star the size of the Sun has used all its hydrogen, it will start using helium in the nuclear reactions at its core, and the star will swell in size to become a red giant.

43 As a red giant cools and shrinks, it becomes a small star called a white dwarf. It is packed tightly with material, but quite small. White dwarfs eventually fade, but can still shine for billions of years.

44 Stars with much lower mass then the Sun will just fizzle out. Once they have run out of hydrogen fuel, they are not big enough to use helium in their reactions, so they dim and cool.

45 There is one enormous dying star that is bigger than the distance from the Sun to Jupiter and back! Mu Cephei (also known as the Garnet Star) shines about 100,000 times more brightly than the Sun.

46 Planetary nebulae are created by some dying stars, but they were named by mistake. When astronomers first spotted them they thought they looked like the gas planets, Jupiter and Neptune. Planetary nebulae contain lots of gas, but no planets.

▲ A dying star blows away layers of dust and gas to form this planetary nebula, called the Helix Nebula.

▶ This chart shows the likely fates of different types of stars found throughout the Universe.

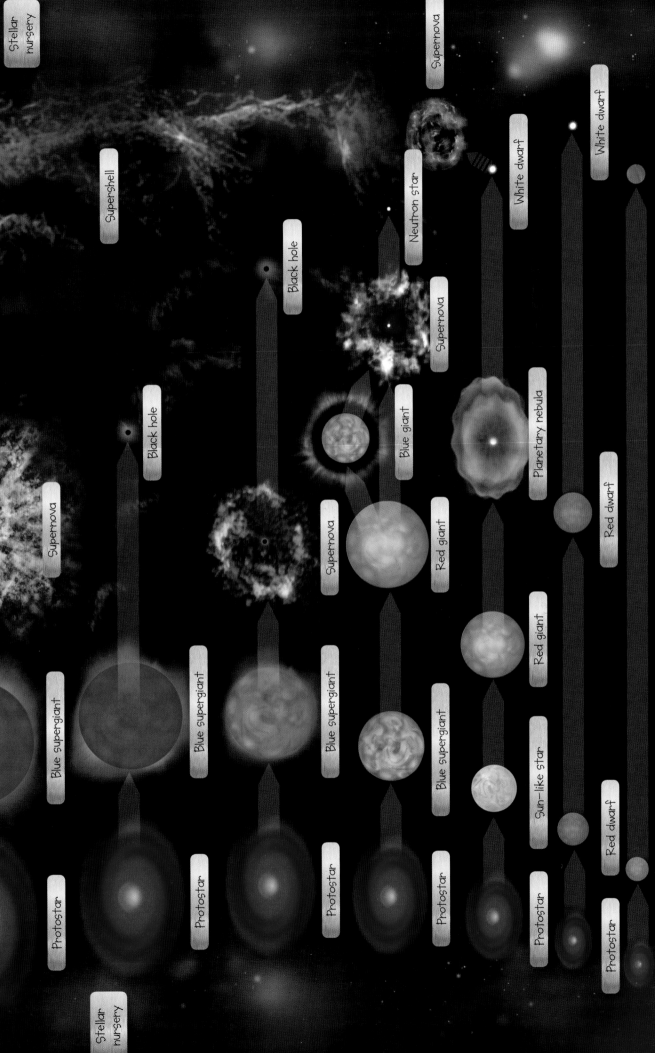

Stunning supernovae

47 Some stars die spectacular and violent deaths through giant explosions. Stars eight or more times more massive than the Sun swell up as they burn all their hydrogen, helium and other elements as fuel. The core of the star collapses in on itself and then much of the star rebounds in a truly gigantic explosion called a supernova.

48 One supernova was so bright, it could be viewed from Earth by day. In 1604, astronomer Johannes Kepler tracked a supernova explosion using just his eyes despite the fact that it was some 20,000 light years away.

▶ Johannes Kepler was able to track his supernova for a full year. Kepler's teacher, Tycho Brahe, had also tracked a supernova in 1572.

◀ This SN1006 supernova remnant is approximately 60 light years in diameter. It is the remains of a white dwarf star, which was ripped apart in a supernova explosion.

I DON'T BELIEVE IT!
Supernovae explosions fling out gas and dust at high speed – as fast as 30,000 kilometres per second.

▼ The Crab Nebula is still expanding at an approximate speed of 1500 km per second.

49 Some supernova remnants can be observed long after the explosion. In 1054, a supernova explosion occurred, which Chinese astronomers called a "guest star". The remains of the supernova, now called the Crab Nebula, can still be seen with a telescope and is about 12 light years wide.

50 The first supernova seen since the invention of the telescope was in 1987. Supernova 1987a occurred in the Large Magellanic Cloud galaxy over 160,000 years ago. Astronomers measured debris from the explosion moving at 30 million kilometres an hour.

51 In 2011, Supernova 2010lt was discovered by a 10-year-old Canadian schoolgirl. Kathryn Aurora Gray was the youngest person ever to discover a supernova.

▶ Kathyrn Aurora Gray (seen here meeting Neil Armstrong) spotted the supernova while looking through images taken by a Canadian telescope.

Neutron stars

52 Some exploding stars leave behind a neutron star. The outer layers of the star blast away, leaving behind an incredibly heavy core. Gravity pulls in surrounding matter and draws the core in on itself, making the star incredibly dense and small. A neutron star's gravity is billions of times stronger than the gravity we experience on Earth.

53 A teaspoon of neutron star might weigh more than one million tonnes. Neutron stars can be about 20–25 kilometres in diameter but can have the mass of two of our Suns.

54 Some neutron stars, called pulsars, spin round thousands of times a minute. Pulsars send out streams of radiation as they rotate. PSR J1748-2446ad, spins 716 times a second – that's 43,000 times per minute!

▲ Some neutron stars may draw in matter from neighbouring stars as well as shooting out long jets of radiation from their centre.

55 Neutron stars can sometimes cause massive energy bursts known as star quakes. They crack their outer surfaces as they move, releasing a burst of energy, which flashes through space. In 2004, neutron star, SGR 1806-20, generated the biggest burst of energy ever measured. In a tenth of a second, it contained as much energy as the Sun gives out in 100,000 years.

QUIZ

1. When was the biggest burst of energy measured from a neutron star?
2. In a neutron star, is gravity thousands, millions or billions times stronger than on Earth?
3. Who discovered the first pulsar?

Answers:
1. 2004 2. Billions
3. Jocelyn Bell Burnell

◀ SGR 1806-20 releases energy in a star quake. The star is only 20 kilometres in diameter and spins rapidly completing a full turn every 7.5 seconds.

▼ Pulsar B1919+21 is located approximately 2280 light years from Earth.

56 The first pulsar found was originally called Little Green Men I. In 1967, a radio astronomer, Jocelyn Bell Burnell, detected a radio signal from space occurring every 1.34 seconds. She called it LGM-1, short for Little Green Men. Instead of being a message from aliens, it turned out to be a pulsar now called PSR B1919+21.

Mysterious black holes

57 Black holes can be formed from the death of massive stars. Stars that have been through a huge supernova still leave a core behind. In some cases, this core collapses in on itself and forms a dense point in space. Astronomers call this a singularity, and it is the centre of a black hole.

58 There's an enormous, mysterious black hole called Sagittarius A✳ at the middle of our galaxy. Astronomers believe it has the same mass as between three and four million Suns. Supermassive black holes, like Sagittarius A✳, are found in the centre of galaxies. The black hole at the centre of the NGC 1277 galaxy is one of the biggest. Scientists estimate its mass to be equal to 17 billion Suns.

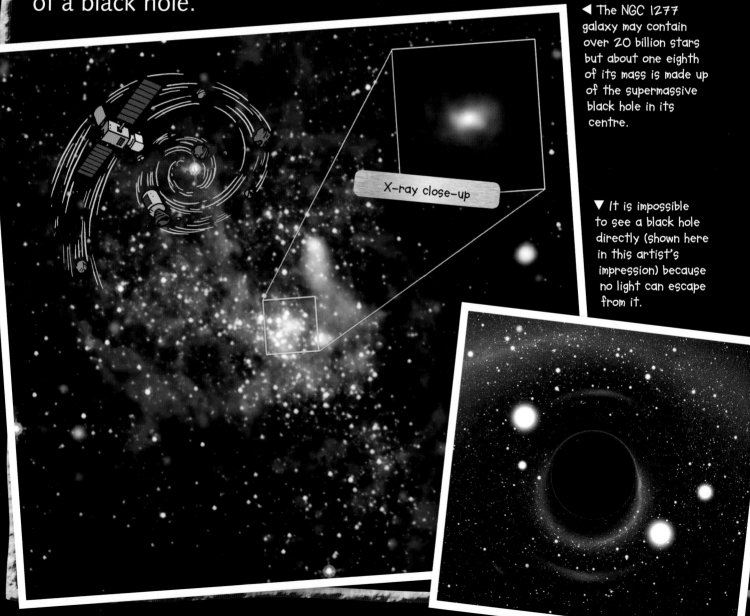

X-ray close-up

◀ The NGC 1277 galaxy may contain over 20 billion stars but about one eighth of its mass is made up of the supermassive black hole in its centre.

▼ It is impossible to see a black hole directly (shown here in this artist's impression) because no light can escape from it.

Star

Black hole

▲ A Sun-like star plunges towards a supermassive black hole.

59 Nothing can escape a black hole because its gravity is so strong. Matter drawn towards it, including planets and stars, passes the event horizon, a point from which it is impossible to escape being pulled inside.

60 Streams of matter shoot away from some black holes. Why this occurs precisely remains a mystery. The supermassive black hole at the centre of the M87 galaxy ejects a stream of hot gas that is an incredible 5000 light years in length.

Star distorting

Black hole

▲ Strong forces distort the star. If it passes too close it will be ripped apart.

Accretion disk

Disrupted star

▲ Matter from the star is drawn towards a black hole and can form a disc of material around the black hole called an accretion disc.

61 Some black holes spin fast. A black hole called GRS 1915+105 lies about 35,000 light years from Earth and is spinning around at incredible speed – between 950 and 1150 times every second.

Particles being ejected

▲ A black hole ejects a massive jet or stream of matter. This can measure many light years in length.

Families of stars

62 **A galaxy is a giant collection of stars.** These are all held together by gravity. Inside even the smallest galaxies are more than a million stars. The biggest galaxies hold many billions of stars. Galaxies also contain large clouds of gas, dust, planets and the remains of old stars.

▲ The two colliding Antennae galaxies (NGC 4038 and NGC 4039) create a spectacular sight. Within 400 million years, they will form a single galaxy.

63 **The biggest known galaxy, IC1101, is 50 times wider than our Milky Way.** It lies 1.07 billion light years away and is around six million light years wide. Scientists estimate that it may contain as many as 100 thousand billion stars.

64 **Occasionally, two galaxies collide, forming lots of new stars.** The Antennae galaxies started colliding a few hundred million years ago. As the two galaxies crash into each other, gas and dust is pressed together. The energy from the collision forms new stars.

▲ I Zwicky 18 galaxy was once thought to be very young. Further studies have discovered it has some faint stars that are as much as 10 billion years old.

65
Galaxies can vary greatly in age. When astronomers first spied I Zwicky 18, they thought it was a young galaxy because most of its stars were only 500 million years old. Galaxy UDFy-38135539 is thought to be over 13.2 billion years old, making it the oldest object scientists have observed in the Universe.

66
There are more than 170 billion galaxies in the Universe. That's 24 galaxies for every person on Earth! As telescopes and other scientific instruments used to look into space improve and reach further and deeper into space, astronomers may find even more.

▼ The Hubble Space Telescope's Deep Field and Ultra Deep Field observations peer back in time to incredibly distant and old galaxies formed relatively shortly after the Big Bang.

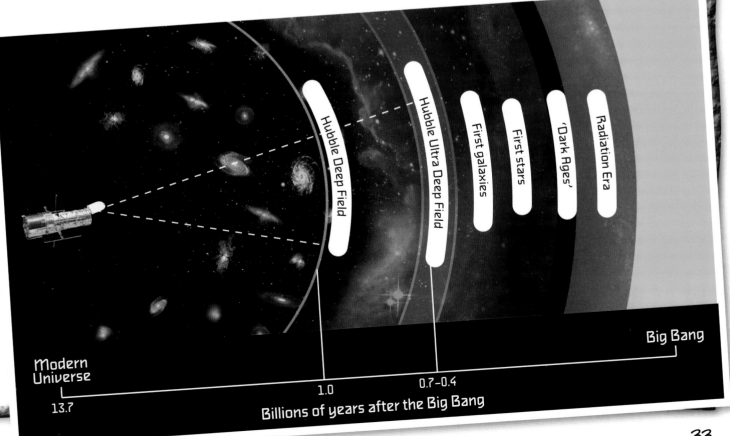

Hubble Deep Field

Hubble Ultra Deep Field

First galaxies

First stars

'Dark Ages'

Radiation Era

Big Bang

Modern Universe

13.7

1.0

0.7–0.4

Billions of years after the Big Bang

Types of galaxy

67 Astronomers group galaxies together according to their shape. Elliptical galaxies form round or oval shapes. They don't rotate much and don't contain many new stars. Spiral galaxies, such as our Milky Way and NGC 253 have plenty of gas and dust for new star formation.

▼ M87 is an elliptical galaxy at least 120,000 light years wide and containing over two trillion stars.

68 Some galaxies are dwarfs, a tiny fraction of the size of the Milky Way. Recent discoveries have shown that lots of little galaxies exist that are jam-packed with stars. These are called ultra compact dwarf galaxies.

▼ NGC 253 galaxy is one of the brightest spiral galaxies visible, and also one of the dustiest, which means lots of stars are formed at a rapid rate.

QUIZ

1. What type of galaxy is NGC 253?
2. Which galaxy contains the most stars: M87 or M60-UCD1?
3. By what name is NGC 6822 galaxy also known?

Answers:
1. Spiral galaxy 2. M87
3. Barnard's Galaxy

69 A newly discovered galaxy called M60-UCD1 is an ultra compact dwarf galaxy. It is just 160 light years wide, but home to as many as 140 million stars. Stars in this galaxy are packed at least 25 times closer than in our part of the Milky Way.

70 Irregular galaxies have no clear shape. Astronomers believe they formed due to a collision with another galaxy some time in the past. As a result, many irregular galaxies have a mix of baby protostars, young stars and old stars.

▲ NGC 6822, also known as Barnard's Galaxy, is an irregular dwarf galaxy about 1.6 million light years away. It contains around 10 million stars, young and old.

71 Around three quarters of all galaxies are spiral galaxies. They have long curved arms and turn around the galaxy's centre, or hub. The shape of the hub may be circular, or if it is more rectangular it is known as a barred spiral.

◄ A barred spiral galaxy has a large number of bright stars running across its centre.

Our home galaxy

72 Our Solar System is part of the huge Milky Way galaxy. Our home galaxy is a spiral around 100–120,000 light years wide. It's about 1000 light years thick except in the bulging centre called the hub, which is around 5–7 times thicker.

▶ Our Milky Way formed over 12 billion years ago.

GALACTIC CORE

ORION SPUR

SOLAR SYSTEM

OUTER RING

73 The Milky Way is part of a collection of more than 30 galaxies called the Local Group. These include Andromeda, a spiral galaxy, the elliptical galaxy M32 and irregular galaxies, such as the Large Magellanic Cloud. Other clusters of galaxies lie throughout the Universe.

CRUX-SCRUTUM

SAGITTARIUS ARM

PERSEUS ARM

75 Like Earth orbits the Sun, our Solar System orbits the centre of the Milky Way. It does so at high speed – around 792,000 kilometres per hour or 220 kilometres every second. Even at this speed, a galactic year (which is the time it takes for the Solar System to complete its orbit) lasts over 225 million years.

74 The Sun is just one of more than 100 billion stars in the Milky Way. Many millions are contained in the central bulge and in the two largest spiral arms, the Perseus arm and the Sagittarius arm.

76 From face–on, astronomers believe the Milky Way looks like a giant Catherine wheel. From its hub, around 27,000 light years across, long spiral arms of stars and gas curve out from the centre.

Seeing stars

77 **Ancient astronomers used just their eyes to spot the stars.** Some ancient astronomers mapped the position and movement of stars in great detail. The Greek astronomer, Hipparchus, made an amazing catalogue of over 800 stars more than 2100 years ago. On a clear night a person can see around 2000 stars in the sky.

▲ Ancient Babylonian astronomers were among the first to produce catalogues of stars they observed, written on clay tablets over 3200 years ago.

78 **Many amateur telescopes have a 10 centimetre aperture.** However, the Gran Telescopio Canarias (GTC) scientific telescope is 100 times as big. A bigger aperture means that more light can be gathered. The GTC is the biggest reflecting telescope in the world. Its aperture measures 10.4 metres wide, enabling it to gather light from really distant galaxies.

▼ Located at an altitude of 2326 metres, the Gran Telescopio Canarias is the largest single optical telescope in the worlld.

79 **Optical telescopes magnify distant objects to bring them closer.** Optical telescopes gather more light than your eye can and focus it to a give a clearer, larger view of distant objects. The first telescopes were invented by Dutch spectacles makers who placed two lenses in a tube in 1608.

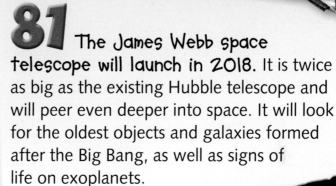

Primary mirror

Secondary mirror

▶ The James Webb's large 6.4-metre-diameter mirror will give the telescope around seven times more light-gathering power than the Hubble.

Sunshield

80 Reflecting telescopes use mirrors instead of lenses. Invented by British scientist, Sir Isaac Newton in 1668, reflecting telescopes focus light by bouncing it off a series of mirrors. It is easier to make big mirrors than big lenses so the biggest optical telescopes used today by astronomers are reflectors.

▼ Sir Isaac Newton's first reflecting telescope used a piece of polished tin-copper metal alloy as a mirror.

81 The James Webb space telescope will launch in 2018. It is twice as big as the existing Hubble telescope and will peer even deeper into space. It will look for the oldest objects and galaxies formed after the Big Bang, as well as signs of life on exoplanets.

I DON'T BELIEVE IT!
The Hubble Space Telescope has taken over 700,000 photos of stars, galaxies and other things in space since it was sent into space in 1990

Patterns in the sky

82 **Stars form patterns in the night sky.** Different people in the past gave these patterns different names. In the 1920s, these were reorganized into 88 different named areas in the night sky, known as constellations. Some are named after characters in ancient myths, such as Hercules and Orion or after animals, such as Leo (lion) or Lupus (wolf).

KEY
1. Cassiopeia – mythical Queen
2. Ursa Major – Great Bear
3. Draco – dragon
4. Cygnus – swan
5. Hydra – water snake

83 **Not all stars can be seen at one time.** As Earth travels on its orbit around the Sun, different stars can be seen at different times of the year. This is why maps of the night sky differ depending on the months or seasons of the year.

▶ This diagram shows how our line of sight alters depending on Earth's movement around the Sun.

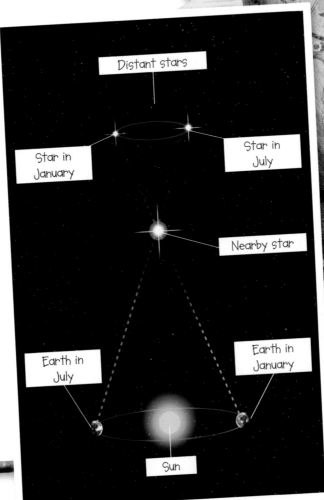

Distant stars

Star in January

Star in July

Nearby star

Earth in July

Earth in January

Sun

▲ This 17th century map of the constellations shows how many were named after mythical people, gods or creatures.

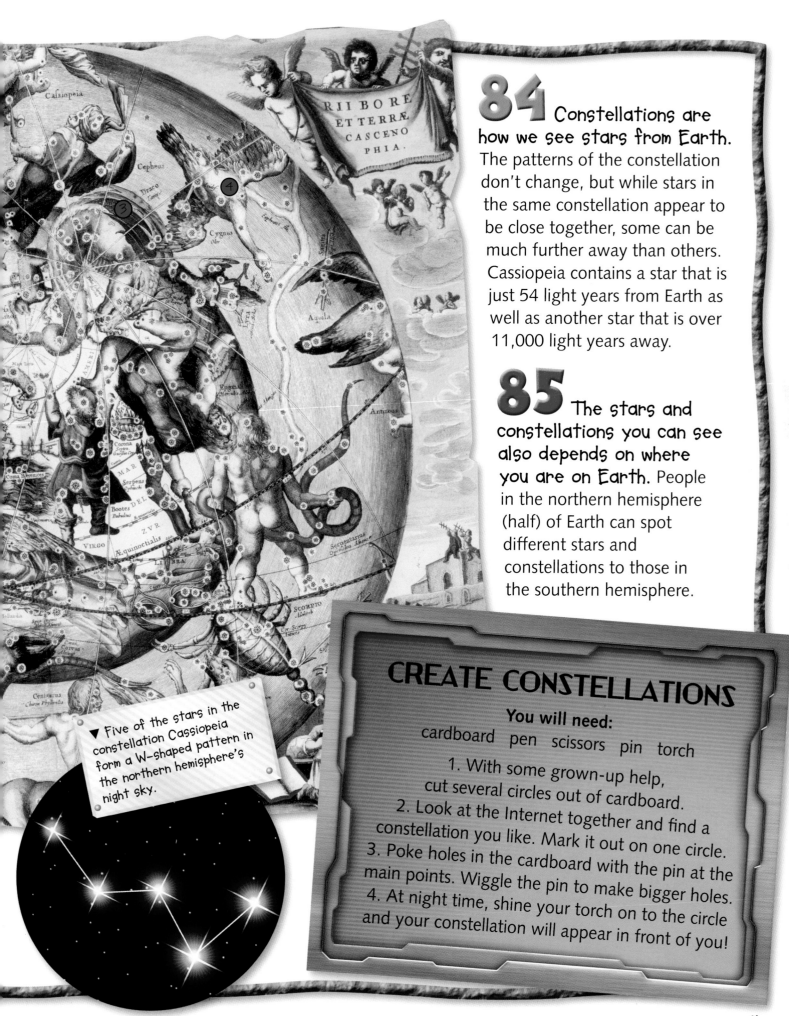

84 Constellations are how we see stars from Earth. The patterns of the constellation don't change, but while stars in the same constellation appear to be close together, some can be much further away than others. Cassiopeia contains a star that is just 54 light years from Earth as well as another star that is over 11,000 light years away.

85 The stars and constellations you can see also depends on where you are on Earth. People in the northern hemisphere (half) of Earth can spot different stars and constellations to those in the southern hemisphere.

▼ Five of the stars in the constellation Cassiopeia form a W-shaped pattern in the northern hemisphere's night sky.

CREATE CONSTELLATIONS

You will need:
cardboard pen scissors pin torch

1. With some grown-up help, cut several circles out of cardboard.
2. Look at the Internet together and find a constellation you like. Mark it out on one circle.
3. Poke holes in the cardboard with the pin at the main points. Wiggle the pin to make bigger holes.
4. At night time, shine your torch on to the circle and your constellation will appear in front of you!

86 Stars and galaxies don't just give off light. Visible light, which travels in waves, is just one form of electromagnetic radiation. Other types exist, such as ultraviolet, which is mostly emitted by young stars and white dwarfs. Instruments capture these waves and tell us more about objects in space.

▲ Since its launch in 1999, the Chandra X-ray Observatory has made many discoveries, including finding neutron stars, black holes and young stars bursting into life.

88 X-rays are given off by stars and other objects hotter than 1 million°C. Neutron stars, hot gas close to black holes and supernovae remnants all give off X-rays, which can be detected by special telescopes, such as the Chandra Observatory.

87 When stars collide or explode as a supernova, they give off bursts of radiation called gamma rays. Gamma rays can contain huge amounts of energy. A major gamma ray burst can release more energy in ten seconds than the Sun will give off in its lifetime.

▶ These two images show the same spiral galaxy using two methods. The top one is a black and white image using visible light only. The bottom one is an X-ray image.

▶ Fermi is a scientific satellite, which carries a telescope to scan the Universe for gamma rays.

▼ The electromagnetic spectrum is the range of frequencies of electromagnetic radiation. It ranges from the high frequencies of gamma rays to the low frequency of radio communication.

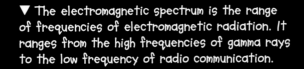

Electromagnetic energy

Gamma ray   X-ray   Ultraviolet

89 Infrared is a type of radiation that can travel through clouds of dust and gas. The Infrared Astronomical Satellite (IRAS) discovered over 300,000 sources of infrared waves from space. Thousands of these were starburst galaxies with new stars forming inside them.

▼ This infrared image of the Andromeda Galaxy was taken by IRAS and is red and orange where the strongest infrared waves are given out, and blue where the weakest are emitted.

▲ The Spitzer space telescope collects infrared waves given off by cooler objects, such as brown dwarf stars and dust at the centre of galaxies.

90 Many objects in space were discovered using radio telescopes. These huge dishes, sometimes as big as 300 metres in diameter, gather signals from large clouds of gas, dust and pulsars. A series of radio telescope dishes working together is called an array.

▼ The ALMA telescope array in Chile features 66 dishes, which can work together. Fifty of these dishes are 12 metres in diameter and weigh 85–115 tonnes each.

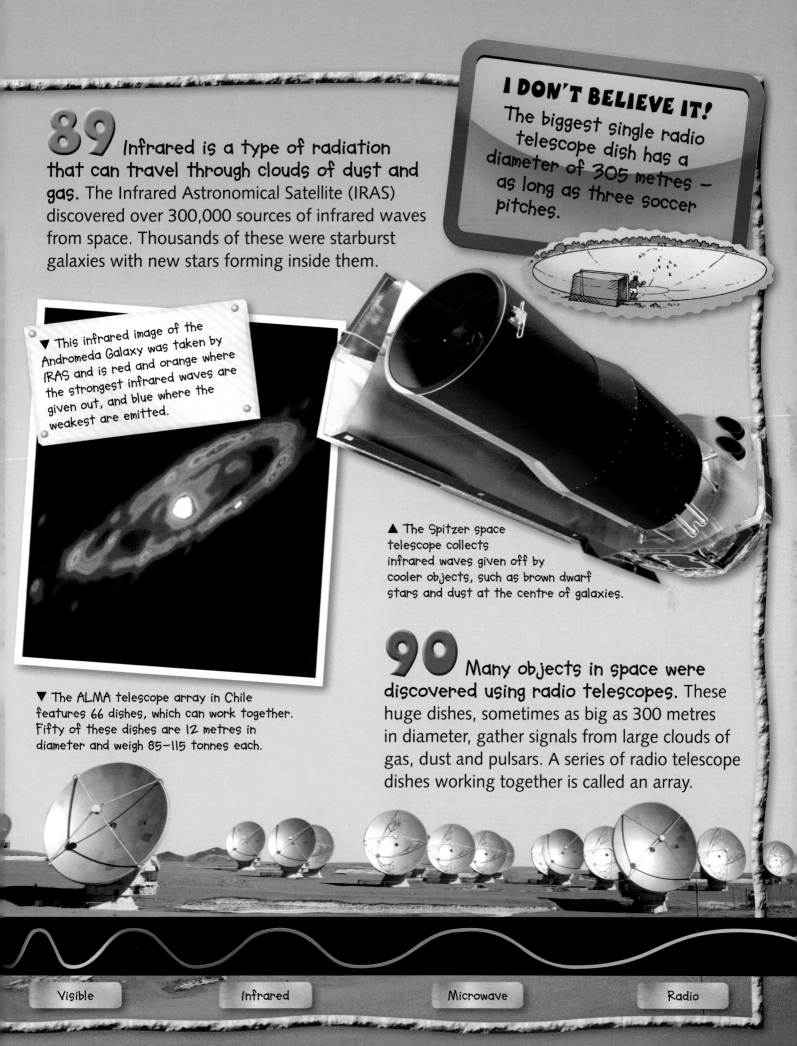

| Visible | Infrared | Microwave | Radio |

New worlds

91 Planets outside the Solar System are called exoplanets. More than 1800 of these have been discovered, since the first one was confirmed in 1992. Planets form from the disc of dust and gas that often swirls around a new star. This could mean many stars have planets orbiting them.

▲ Six exoplanets orbit around the Kepler-11 star. Its closet planet, Kepler b, is just one tenth of the distance that Earth is from the Sun.

◀ Kepler orbits the Sun and seeks out stars with planets orbiting them. It has already helped discover over 1000 exoplanets.

▲ The exoplanet HD 189733 b is a little bigger than Jupiter, but orbits its star in just 2.2 days.

92 One exoplanet's atmosphere possibly rains glass, not water. The conditions on HD 189733 b exoplanet are very hostile, with extreme temperatures and high winds. The atmosphere contains particles of silica – the material from which glass is made.

▲ The habitable zones are shown in green around three different types of star (from top): a hot star, a Sun-like star and a cooler star.

93 The solar system is just one star system. Five planets are known to orbit the Kepler 186, a star with around half the mass of the Sun. At least seven planets have been found in the Gliese 667c star system.

94 Scientists are excited by finding exoplanets in the 'goldilocks zone' or habitable zone. This is where exoplanets, like Gliese 667Cc, orbit within an area that is close enough to their star to be the right temperature for life to form. Exoplanets in the goldilocks zone may have water and the other things life needs to exist.

95 Exoplanets can take hours to travel around their star or thousands of years. Exoplanet Fomalhaut b, is believed to take around 2000 years to complete an orbit of its star. WASP-12b exoplanet only takes 26 hours to complete its journey around its star.

▼ This illustration shows a possible exoplanet, orbiting the Gliese 581 star, which is around 20 light years from Earth.

96 No extraterrestrials or aliens have been found... yet. Many scientists believe that the Universe is so vast that life must exist elsewhere. Our knowledge of the Universe is constantly changing with new discoveries being made every year.

▲ Kepler 186f is about 10 percent bigger than Earth, and takes 129.9 days to complete an orbit around its star.

97 Only one human–made object has ever left the Solar System. The *Voyager 1* space probe was launched in 1977 and left the Solar System in 2014. Although it is racing along at a rate of 1.5 million kilometres per day, it will still take thousands of years to reach another star system.

98 Exoplanet Kepler 186f was discovered in 2014. Scientists are excited because it is approximately the same size as Earth, and the right distance away from its star to potentially support life.

▼ *Voyager 1* is about 19 billion kilometres from the Sun and left our Solar System in 2014.

99 Alien life might be quite different to Earth. Some planets have heavier atmospheres, which would support enormous flying creatures, for example, while on other planets living things might not even need water or oxygen to survive outer space.

▶ Tardigrades (one millimetre in size) are the first animals to survive exposure in space, surviving sub-zero temperatures, solar radiation and no oxygen.

100 Scientists have sent many welcome messages into space. Four space probes (*Pioneer 10* and *11*, and *Voyager 1* and *2*) carry gold plaques or discs showing pictures of humans and our place in the Solar System. Radio telescopes, such as the giant Arecibo dish in Puerto Rico, have also beamed messages into space. Earth is still waiting for a reply.

▲ *Pioneer 11* was launched in 1973. It was built to last 21 months, but kept sending information back to Earth until 1995.

▲ Voyager's gold disc contained technical images showing how to play its record on the other side, as well as Earth's location from 14 stars.

I DON'T BELIEVE IT!
The gold discs carried by *Voyager 1* and *2* could also be played to reveal sounds of Earth as well as greetings in 55 different languages.

Index